THE
LAMENT
Selected Poems and Prose

ERCELL H. HOFFMAN

Outskirts Press, Inc.
Denver, Colorado

Outskirts Press, Inc.
http://www.outskirtspress.com

ISBN: 978-1-4327-4346-8

Library of Congress Control Number: 2011931563

Outskirts Press and the "OP" logo are trademarks belonging to Outskirts Press, Inc.

PRINTED IN THE UNITED STATES OF AMERICA

Table of Contents

My Other Self

While upon a dream I slumbered
running to escape loneliness
fighting to escape injuries
I fell deeply and softly upon all I'd known — aloneness.
And in reality I hear cries of needing then rejection
longings and the sound of footsteps rushing away.
Then I'm filled with wonder — wondering and drifting
shifting and the sifting to weed out all that which is
irrelevant
and all that remains is the sifter and me.
Wondering as before and drifting into some far-off land
which appears familiar but unexplored.
And suddenly all but that which now exists is gone.
On this early morn I sit in the bliss of solitude.
I am surrounded at noonday by the sound of machinery
while the sun's rays beam impersonally down upon me
and a soft breeze stirs, sputtering litter here and there
impersonal faces turning to glimpse an unimportant
figure
none caring.
And all warmth comes naught but from the sun.
Today I summon my thought to recollect upon my
yesterdays
and you are there.
And now I'm haunted by my own failure to understand.
Yet I understand too well.
I am pained by the simplicity of it all.
Pained because you thought me not so good
and pained because at the height of my love
you shunned me and turned away.
I've not by choice gone to another
aware, more often than wise, of you.

And now I'm engulfed by a state of serenity
and time leaves naught but time for living
time for hearing and time for seeing.
I feel a close relation to all that which is nothing
like oil spilled upon the ground
waiting to be walked upon
until it, too, becomes a part of the earth.
On this day veils of clouds cover the sun
as veils of myths hide me from truth.
And what is truth
but that which is accepted in the light of thought as
divine.
I embark upon this plane seeking that light.
This midafternoon I meditate
but in too short a period to reach the depth of my own
existence
and go wandering about to join the masses.
Within the canyon of my mind in a state of
semiconsciousness
I climbed a mountain of hard rock and stone.
Only one path would lead me there.
And one day when I found that age had taken away my
vigor
I became frantic and over and over I tried.
And from out of nowhere you appeared and showed me
the way.
In full consciousness I observe this evolutionary status
as a wheel.
I am a spoke within that wheel
And from a hidden small dark corner of the universe
I tear away the darkness to move into an ever-shining
light.

In my mind's eye I see mountains of doubt crumble
and I see the fullness of you unfold before me.
When we are close
I feel the purity of me melting and running into you
and I seem to lose myself.
But at eventide all my incapabilities come to surface
and I feel less capable.
First I am aroused with great passion.
No sooner than I began to feed upon it
it vanishes, as smoke into the air.
Again I return to whence I started — alone.

I Fall in Love too Easily

To reach out and touch
to be frightened by the feel
or to encircle one's self within an invisible shield
are only cowardly acts.
But to touch and to love the feel
to break that invisible shield
to witness the joy and pain
that learning to love always brings
is the true beginning from which self-insight springs.
Or is it really best to stay within that shell
where no pain or heartache can ever dwell
and where disappointment can never be
because hope is as bare as a fruitless tree?
By a single attempt to break that shell
one is suddenly confronted with all kinds of hell.
But an ego covered by too much shade
when in the sunlight, suddenly fades.
And soon it will find itself to be
just another branch upon a huge tree.
And when the wind blows
it shakes like the rest
with nothing to distinguish it as the best.
So it finds itself, like thousands of others
that when the storm comes there are no covers.
But when we leave our shell
only then can we dwell
where the sunlight shines
and by chance we might happen upon
moments which are sublime.
And only those moments help us to know
that when the winter grounds are covered with snow
seasons do change and maybe again we'll grow.

Untitled

If just for one day man could live
without doubt or fear
it would strengthen him and mankind
for that day and all the year.
But time waits not for anyone
who has by fate come 'long
while it buries the weak in sorrow
the strong continue to roam.
With gallant bright spirit they trace
the speeding tracks of time
not knowing what lies before them
not stopping to look behind.
For men of brave set out to change
the wrongness of their time
fearlessly doing that which is right
with hope the light will shine.
Shine on bright souls of un-dauntless courage
for in the light you see
those who have fallen along the side
in swollen rivers of grief.
And seeing light gives hope
to weaklings who have fallen . . . Like me.

The Factory

She has large, clear eyes and smiles a lot.
When alone in her thoughts, she sometimes cries.
But no one ever knows
for she hides her tears and guards them as precious
falling stones
upon which she will one day climb
and no one will know the secret of how she reached her
height.
In the big factory with many people she is lonely.
One boy she met and she liked his eyes.
They were bright.
But in the spring he went away.
When years had passed, she met a man whose hair was
gray
his eyes looked tired and she was tired and she
understood.
In the factory are many people
whose eyes are indifferent
and whose smiles are like plastic
stretched across their mouths
and their greetings are like sounds they have learned.
Several times within a day they pass each other
and repeat the sound — without thinking.
Some wear bright and colorful garments at the factory.
And they do not speak to those who do not.
They hold their heads high
But no sparks are in their eyes.
They, at the factory, are perfectly groomed
yet they do not have the look of freshness.
They walk in hurried steps
yet there is no sense of urgency.
But she with eyes

made clear and bright by her tears that no one sees
is not like the others.
Her hours at the factory are spent alone.
She hears no conversations that interest her.
The ideas of those who speak are different from hers.
Her companions are her thoughts, her dreams, .her
hopes, and her books
some of whose authors she holds in high esteem
for they have accomplished in their way what she hopes
to in hers.
In the confines of the factory
when her thoughts cannot be silenced she picks up her
pen and speaks.
Sometimes she is left with a sense of weariness
much like the tiredness she perceives around her.
And she puts down her pen.
But she has spoken.

On Life

If I would write a poem on sadness
I would look upon the face of a workman
who finds no pleasure in his work.
If I would write a poem on deception
I would look at him
who has not delved deeply within his soul in search of
truth.
And I would find it among men and women of all faith.
Were I to focus my thoughts on happiness and pleasure
I would gaze upon the babes of youth
while they busy themselves doing little great things.
Were I to take a glimpse at warmth
I would look into the eyes of one who love has come to
rescue
from the shackles of disappointment
from the threshold of despair
and from closed walls of loneliness.
 And in those eyes I would find a light
that shines as a soft moon
and feel the sublimity of a small running brook from the
vast sea
that flows beneath a log.
 And in their depth I would see a shadow
as looking into a deep dark well on a day when the sun
is touched upon it.

Nullified Existence

Inhale. Exhale
a frown behind each smile.
Tears and laughter between trivial moments.
There's a conscious mistrust of all things tangible
and most especially, the intangible.
Sleep, dream, and awaken unutterably forsaken and
alienated.
Empathy destroyed by anxiety
love strangled by frustration
hope destroyed by marked limitation
Ah, and an ache to feel the need of someone!
To contend with inconsistent fragmentations of an
unknown self
with vague glimpses just beyond the mentality to grasp
the substance that constitute a whole self.
Searching in stand-still mannerisms
caught up, leaving no time to bury the fear
that it would lead to greater understanding and
wisdom.
Bounded by trivial moments
whose impact is great upon the consciousness.
And at a time when nothing is certain
renders only those moments worth living and reliving.
Only then is life's struggle not one.
Inhale . . . exhale awaiting a trivial moment.

Knowing You

To know such golden moments
as those I've shared with you
is to feel the kind of splendor
that stays forever new!

The Lonely House

This is a lonely house.
Everyone has deserted it.
As the hours pass
she sits quietly
never bothered by intruders wanting to steal a peek into
her half-opened door.
Though she hears every sound for miles around
laughter, music, and sometimes fears
the sounds of footsteps hurrying by
and cars speeding up and down the street
None aware that she stands motionless
silently aching to feel the entrance of some new soul.
Waiting for when her walls will contain within
the self-same joys she hears from without
awaiting the day when she'll embrace two lovers' hearts
and the noise of a loving family.
And the day she'll be left alone again
to await the return of other joyful noisemakers.
Her panels are bare except for a portrait or two.
A calendar hangs on the wall
reflecting the month, day, and year.
The hanging drapes move with the autumn breeze.
A chair sits empty by the foot of the bed
longing to hold some friendly visitor.
Her silent cries ring out aloud
"Save me, O Lord, the ticking time of eternity alone to
witness thee!"

The Speechless Pen

Writing pen, O writing pen, what have you to say?
Have you been down so long you've gone speechless?
Have you not a breath of hope to offer me from your
long-pointed mouth?
Are there not a few little words that may ring
to make this sad heart sing?
Oh, please, dear pen, speak to me gently to let me know
you are still alive!

Memories

Oh, how well do I remember
the month was one past December.
The rain fell softly in the night
when my heart from me did flight.
I know the day, the hour too
when your first kiss fell like the dew.
With passion real, warm, and deep
that within my heart, it still does keep.
And oh, how fast my cares did grow
like melting ice or balls of snow.

Thinking of You

Last night I dreamed of you
holding me close to your heart
as you once did from the start.
Like mighty arms of war you fought with yours
to bring me near
and then with lips as soft as a tear
you kissed me.

This Holiday

Today I'll be lonely and a little blue too
for all that I do
will be without you.
And this whole holiday season
I'll be trying to forget
all those happy times we spent without any regrets.
Although you'll never hear these words
straight from my heart
I'll be thinking of you, darling,
when the old year ends and the new one starts.

What the Hell If I Dream

Hollow inside I'm wondering
hoping to soon happen upon that something to erase my
wanting.
But until then what the hell if I dream
and go backward in time to recall the moments when
we walked
hand in hand by the ocean front
or sat at water's edge
Or the morning after our fight.
I came to you.
Without speaking
you opened the door and went back to bed.
Without speaking
I sat closely beside you and felt the warmth of passion
Lifted the covers that covered you
and placed myself close beside you.
Without speaking
you reached over and took me in your arms
drawing me closer without speaking.
This whole night, my love,
I will devote to the memories of you
and hope that one day I'll know again
those passionate moments we shared
  with hope that time will never erase them.
Oh what the hell if I dream!
Only then can I feel you
hear your voice from a distance as I fight sleepiness.
Loving the poem you're reading
but wishing for the moment to come quickly
when we'd make our own.
Quickly, before only dream is mine.
Just then you would touch me

kiss me awake and we'd make our poem.
Oh what the hell if I dream!
Only then can I bring you back
to see your eyes
feel your hands
hear your voice and kiss your lips.
Oh, what the hell if I dream!

Deviled Angel

This morning, before the break of dawn
It started raining.
I awoke, feeling half asleep.
And each drop I heard reminded me of you.
I turned and pulled the covers snug
and fell asleep again, in love with you.
Oh, that beguiling angel
who brings me messages and rest upon my soul
As heaven had bestowed her!
And her presence, I cannot ignore.
She awakens me at any hour of the night
in the hurry and rush of day.
. She corners me and whispers silently your love for me
and mine of you.
In conversation she interrupts me
to remind me of you
making me appear a blundering fool in the eyes of
others.
For they do not hear what I hear.
Their hearts are not pierced with a spirit so beguiled.
And as one who never encountered reason or wisdom I
welcome her.
Entrenched, I listen with intrigue
and willingly succumb to the melody and rhapsodies of
love
she brings from you
and when she's gone, I live in a state of death until her
return.

Caring

The sun that shines above the pines
that grow so tall so strong
to my broken heart it seems to say
"You shouldn't stay broke so long."
Her rays so bright
till in the night her face lay plainly bare
and seems to say still without doubt
"I care, I care, I care!"

A Dream

Had a bad dream last night
couldn't half sleep
kept thinking about your love
I couldn't keep.
Was there something I could've done
to make you stay
or was it just the Lord's will you had to go away?
I loved you all I could Heaven knows I did
I just didn't know what to please you with.
But since you've been gone I want to know
if there was something about me
that made you have to go.
As hard as I try I just can't forget
how much I liked you from the first day we met.
I'll just keep thinking
and maybe one day I'll know
just what it was that made you have to go.

Your Love Is Like the Wind

So completely, so fully your smiles, your hellos and all your . . .
this feeling cannot be condensed to words.
 There are none complete enough nor grand enough
none so dear to portray the magnitude of . . .
There are no words that rhyme
however sweet or refined to convey these heartfelt . . .
and to simply say, "I love you" would leave too much unsaid
because "I love you" cannot tell all that I feel.
Yet more than other words I might say it comes, perhaps, closer.
I'll say it again, "I love you, my angel."
Yes, my angel, for you are the gift of God.
Your smile holds for me water
made sweet with the freshness of realness
and it sits like a rose upon your lips
a rose I feel and fresh water I drink each time I kiss them.
Your hellos ring with a melody that goes beyond the ear
to reach a deeper part of self
that self that receives naught but beauty and truth.
No, my angel, words were not meant
were not made to say these things most dear
for they are like the winds we feel
but cannot see and cannot touch
though they kiss and embrace us and make melodies in our ears.

The Memory of You

If the passion of one kiss would continue to live
if the newness of charm would not grow old
if the warmth of a touch could always remain
happiness could never be lost.
The music and shrills of laughter
the ceaseless chattering
the whining of the babe's discontent
the leaves of the palms swinging carelessly with the
afternoon breeze
the sun's gleaming light upon its branches
in the midst of winter
the red roofing across the way
covering the tall, huge building—all remind me of you.

My Sunshine

I've tried to show how much it means
to have you always near;
without your warmth I'm afraid
I'll drown with every tear.
As evening comes the night grows cold
to lead my heart astray.
Still I find with a warn
you leave me late each day.
May I please have the chance to see your shining face
then I'll know, without a doubt, that I can win this race!

Bygones to Sorrow

Time alone helps ease the pain of having lost you.
My days are filled with anticipation of the night
when I'll meet with someone new . . .
or, perhaps, chat with a long-lost friend.
Soon I'll not remember to wonder if you are home,
neither will I glimpse where you might be.
Soon I'll forget how much I love you
and how I long to be near.
Soon, my darling, soon!

A Summer Night

A lovely summer night
The stars were shining bright
No cares at all
Except for each other.
You and I and bliss
An occasional kiss
And maybe we might embrace.

Thank You

A beautiful pearl, indeed!
As delicate as a human heart.
I'll be careful not to break it
and shall never lose it.

My Friend

Many years have passed
since I felt the inner yearning for your love.
Though time has not erased the warmth that permeates
when I think of how gradually
we grew closer than we ever were.
Comforting to know that love never dies.
Though never with the thought of a "passing fancy"
did I fancy you.
Little then did I realize your infinite charm.
When time no longer is
I will still love you.

I Love You

Whatever is there that keeps us apart?
My burning heart becomes soothed by the mere
awareness of you.
My empty arms become filled
as I draw near you in my dream.
Cold mornings are made warm with the thought of you.
In others I look for you.
If your presence is vague, I go astray.
If it is strong, of course, I stay.
Frantically I search the eyes of new faces
to see your gleaming look.
Patiently I listen to hear the controlled eagerness of your
voice.
And vainly I await his touch.

Moody

No mood for talk
no mood for song
I want to go where I belong.
The hours here are much too long
for me to think that this is home.
Someplace there must be, for sure,
where I can rest my head for cure.
The spinning waves about my brain
for your love they do proclaim.
Come lay closely about my breast
so this weary head may rest.

Love Song

You feed the hunger of my innermost soul
and your kisses quell the raging madness within me.
In your arms, the softness of heaven enfolds me
while I cease to know the loneness that dwells within
me.
A multitude of voices sing gleefully the song of love
and I feel you stirring inside me
like a whirlwind that stirs the root of a seaweed, and
heaven trembles.
When we are parted there remains something
that links us together.
Measures in distance loses significance
for there is none
and when that something *is* weakened
by my own weakness
shadows of death hover about me
and I become a lone ship in the midst of an ocean of vast
depth without sails.
But when we are one, I ride, again, upon the waves of
eternity.

Stay, Heart, Stay

I can't stop loving you
and won't keep trying.
I'll wait till the end of time.
That might seem long
but it isn't at all
if in the end you'll be standing there, tall.
You've tried, I know, to turn me away
but something within my heart keeps saying, "Stay,
heart, stay."
The day will come, my darling, I know
when you will want me too.
That's why I must obey my heart
when it says what it does about you.
I saw perhaps a glimpse of it
when you looked in my eyes
for love is something, oh, my dear,
when present, cannot hide.

By the Sea

Here we are walking in the sand beside the sea.
And I'm neither torn with grief nor sorrow.
There is though a strangeness about it all.
I can feel it.
Together we have come to my secret place
at an hour when the sea is calm.
Her waves wash upon the shore in a harmony all its
own.
I do not know the sound which calls me unto her
nor do I know the song she sings
but when I part with her
the arrow which bow into my heart
loses its power to sting and I bleed contentedly.

My Love

My love, I cannot sleep needing you like this.
I cannot rest.
Instead, I close my eyes and hear a hundred voices
While drifting into dream lender's silence.
I hear muffled drums drumming
and I awake, needing you.
This morning came and I cannot think straight
needing you like this.
I cannot focus my thoughts.
They keep drifting to you.
Your arms, your hands I like so well
Your lips, you use them so effectively
sending sensational heat waves over me
Oh! my love
I cannot think straight needing you like this.
Instead, I see your eyes, your hair
and now there's a swelling in my throat.
I did not sleep last night or the night before.
The last time I slept I recall
need awakened me
and when I opened my eyes
you were there beside me.

Yesterdays

Notebooks of love letters
remind me of the days
when I gazed upon the sun
to feel her loving rays.
Now those days are gone
while my heart has ceased to beat
for the precious day I see you
to stand beneath your feet.
Strange, I know, it may seem
you are now no more my dream
but the same as water is to a stream
you stand tall amidst my scheme.

Heartbreak

Would I could die of heartbreak this flesh had rotten
while my soul dance betwixt the heaven.
Give me thee thou grave of rest
that I may know in mine youth peace and serenity.
Save this heart of young
solemn hours of secluded loneliness
that it may not curse the hands of destiny that hath set
my fate.

The Meeting of Souls

You are the height of my tallest dream
like a torrent heat wave
rushing throughout my body.
My soul rejoices with your touch.
Beyond the ground and sea,
Flying as free as birds
dancing in fleeting harmony
as gracefully as fish swam the sea.

The Rosebud to a Bee

Suddenly the need to feel your wings around me is here
again
When not long ago
I marveled over your departure.
I felt myself free of the sweet pollen you left upon me
I beheld life lovingly and kissed the sunlight.
I am reminded of another season
when my petals were open wide to the air and sunlight
then died slowly with the winter snow.
Left bare
without even a stem to hold me
from falling atop the ground.
Had I been heavy enough to sink
if no further than beneath a crust of dirt
or if a single leaf had fallen to cover me
the winter rains may not have frozen me.
Only mother earth knew of my loneness.
Only she swallowed the moisture left within my
wrinkled bud.
This time to her will I lay open my heart wide
and for none but her will I blossom in spring
for in the end only she will contain me.

Only a Dream

More intoxicating than wine you affect me.
Like an overdrunken lover
I sit intoxicated with memories of you.
Then I fall asleep and become haunted by your
nearness.
I awake with a hangover of passionate lovemaking
And with a dream I live.

Nervous

My heart beats rapidly
my emotions are at the highest peak.
Everyone and everything annoys me.
The sounds on the radio
like the grinding of steel.
I'm at such unrest
while waiting for the moment when you'll knock quietly
on the door.
At what minute
related to what hour will you come?
How much longer must I wait?
Already, until the sound of the dead echoed in my ear
until my only consolation was to chat with nature's
leaves
that grow from her branches in the stillness of the night
until my soul left my body in quest for yours.
The end of time. Let it be now!

Never Without You

A day never ends without the thought of you.
Few nights pass when you are not my dream.
I speak your name and I'm void of apathy.
I look into your eyes and a spell of serenity engulfs me.
I touch your hand and become nearest to Heaven.

Loving You

I see your hands, your fingers, moving slowly
stirring your coffee.
You are aware that I am noticing
and I feel a sense of shyness that passes on to you.
You cover it well with boldness.
Your lips
I watch them closely
to see them curve around your words.
I feel the coyness in your silence.
My unconcealable desire to kiss your lips
reminds you to tell me I have no restraint.
I wish I didn't.
Then nothing could stop me
And space would not separate us.

Without Love There's Nothing – A Tribute to Love

No thought worth speaking
no need worth wanting
no deed worth doing
no life worth living without love.
Love is the cause of motivation
the source of creation.
Without it all is void and meaningless.
Love is the missing element
in lives filled with despair, loneliness, sickness, and
grief.
It is the thing sought after by criminals
the thing longed for by the insane.
Without love there is no power left for reasoning
no cause left for living.
Love is all there is to salvage man's heart and soul
all there is to save doom and corruption.
Only love can save despair, loneliness, criminals, the
sick, and the insane.
Only love makes life worth living!

This Afternoon

This afternoon, my love
I'll allow myself the luxury and pleasure
of dreaming of a love that might have been
had we not been who we are.
I'll reflect and recall my thoughts upon first seeing you
first seeing your face.
My eyes moved downward to your wait
and past your masculine thighs to your handsome feet.
Suddenly I had to run
for then I knew how much I loved you.
I turned my back to you
and forced myself to keep my eyes away
else I could not predict what might be.
And I thought how impossible it was
that eyes such as mine could perceive someone such as
you
standing before me.
My heart raced to reach the speed of my thoughts.
Perspiration spilled from my pores
and I knew then how much I loved you.
Yes, my love
I shall dream this afternoon
of a love which from the start I knew could not blossom.
Though our hearts and souls met and still do cling,
we had to keep our bodies separate apart from our
thoughts.
Still in my sweetest reveries you are there
to fill the emptiness of my heart with love.
Oh, sweet love which might have been
had we not been who we are.

Just Name the Place and Time

I'll meet you anywhere
just name the place and time
and never will I ask your promise
to be forever mine.
If I found the courage to call upon you
what then should I say?
That I love you
though you don't know me nor do I know you?
That I want you?
That I was just thinking of you and thought I'd give you
a ring?
Oh, by the way, you don't know my name?
That my heart throbs to be near you, anywhere at all?
I looked and found your number
by your name, I chanced to hear
and with the thought of using it
I'm struck with sudden fear.
Oh, darling, my darling, though I can't come nearer,
alas, I love passing you and repeating to myself as I
pass,
"I love you, I love you, I love you!"
I love the way you look at me and I at you.
Oh, God in heaven on this earth what must I do?
Oh, God in heaven, please answer me true.
What on this earth must I do?

Lost to the Moment

All mine to enjoy
the memories of you.
Sitting across the breakfast table
seeing your face through the brightness of Sunday
morning's sunlight.
Listening to my heart speak of last night's ecstasies.
I've been rude to almost everyone
since missing your call.
I remember. I haven't called your name.
I've been unfair.
The next time I speak to you
the first thing I'll say will be your name.
I've missed you to the point of
whatever it is that lends the feeling of the ultimate
height of passion.
So perfect is the feeling of being above the absolute!
It's all so clear
I can't believe you're just a dream
a dream I dreamed so many years ago.
When I'm with you so perfectly at ease am I.
I'm now dreading the moment
when you'll want to become intimate
and I know I won't have to think of a kind way to say,
"No."
It's wonderful, anticipating your touch.
I wish I wasn't dreaming!
What am I thinking, did you say?
I'm thinking how I can imprint upon my brain
every feature of your face
because I want to see you fully before me
When you're gone.
Your forehead

and just how far your hair grows upon it
the shape of your eyebrows, your eyes
but looking into them
I become lost to the moment and I forget.
Your mouth
I see how perfectly your mustache curves above your
lip
and your cheeks.
I only know their softness.
I'm thinking how beautiful
and how precious is the beginning of love
when, without knowing, we only feel.
I feel passion sweep throughout me like a cool summer
breeze
thinking, trying to remember if it's like anything I've felt
before.
Then I look into your eyes
and become lost to the moment.

Springtime

This morning I saw the first sign of spring.
Long skinny clovers
reaching up from beneath cracked cement
to get a breath of air
to unfold their beauty to the light.
It brightened my day!

The Institution

A bell ringing awakens you.
The lights all go on.
You rise, and maybe you'll wash your face
and if there's a sparkle of hope, you brush your teeth
and comb your hair.
Like cattle
you gather into the hall.
After morning medication you light up a cigarette
if you have one or can bum one.
Either way it doesn't matter.
You form a line to go to breakfast; careful—no pushing!
Or you go to the back of the line.
There, everyone's always starved. The medicine makes
you hungry.
You eat, like it's your last meal because that's all you
have.
You gather in the day hall where you'll wait till lunch
and after lunch you wait for dinner.
If there's an empty seat you'll crawl into it and sleep
just to forget the hands on the clock you watch so
closely on the big wall.
You rush to dinner
and after dinner, evening snack just before bed.
Just before day it all starts over again.

A Question of Life

When man is dying does he fight to save his life?
Or does he accept death as his inevitable course?
He lives only if he values life
and only if his living is not a state of death.
Today my life is in question.
Have I the courage and the knowledge to save it?
Courage that gives way to will
and knowledge that shows the way?
How long have I to wait upon an answer?
And who, but I, can answer?
Living death is that slow process that comes with loss of
hope, desire, and ambition
Or life which comes with defiance of death is my choice
now to make.

No Time

Ain't got no time to be caught in a bind.
Every act must count if it ain't but an ounce.
What I have to do is lay a foundation
'cause what I tend to do is to build a relation.
One that can stand the ups and downs
one that will grow and won't fall to the ground.
One that won't give way to trouble that infests the day
and one that is safe from thieves who come by night.
So you with your woman just let me be
before only the earth can hold you or me.
'Course I ain't the kind to raise no fuss
'bout some gal you had before us.
Just make up your mind and don't make no show
'cause sure as I'm talking someone's got to go.
Now I ain't saying that it can't be me.
All I'm saying is take me completely or let me be.

My Child

Yes, my child, you asked me how you got here.
You were conceived from desire and grew on longings.
When I thirsted to drink the passion from your father's
lips
your quivering inside let me know he'd not gone.
When I searched the faces of passersby
with hope of seeing his
it was your steady growth which lent me comfort that
he was there.
And when the day came when I could not live without
him
you were born unto me.
I saw his eyes, kissed his lips . . . played with his nose.
My child, you are the gift of months of longing
and the drink that quenches my thirst for love.

Alone to Wonder

What, O God, will satisfy this craving at the root of
these desires?
Something that burns like coal sits flaming upon my
soul
seeking to find an open door.
It sends my mind in a whirlwind of dusk
retaining nothing of all I've held fast.
It has led me alone on this vast plane to seek an escape.
What lies between here and heaven
between here and hell
or is this one and if so, which?
What will unfold within the minute
the hour or the end of eternity?
For what purpose has this soul upon this plane?
Have I some duty to perform; if so, what?
In the darkest hour I have spoken to Thee
to hear but an echo of my voice.
To Thee I have given my life
only to receive a voiceless rejection.
I have sought peace
and in my grandest illusions, have found it.
In my hour of despair
I have cried out
"O Lord, why hast Thou borne me?"
There was no answer.
I have begged of Thee to take away my misery
yet it remains my closest companion.
Thou hast set before me
a universe of mankind, yet not one to comfort me.
What brutal sin have I committed
and what anonymous laws have I broken
To be left alone to wonder?

The Birth of a Poem

A poem is born to the poet as the dream is to a sleeper.
It is welcomed by the soul as the early morn its dew.
Its nourishment is no less than is the pollen left on the
bud by the life-giving bee.
Like a blossoming flower the soul is relieved.
It is bathing in nature's sunlight.
It's rolling with the speediest clouds.
It's the stillness of the earth beneath.
It's awareness of sounds, feelings, and the strength of
emotions.
It is the gathering of love's resources.
It's boundless, limitless.

Fleeting Moments

Countless times I have been lifted
by the lightheartedness of being in love.
Innumerable times I have fallen into the dungeon of
despair
where life held little promise of my ever rising.
I'll say that next time
I'll do but more to contain my feelings.
Someway I must find the way around that trap that lay
amidst ecstasy.
When day breaks she releases her wings
to leave me sorrowed in thoughts of fleeting yesterdays.
I cannot grasp nor entertain very long the mere idea of
her.
As the winds who gently whisper
humming sweet nothings in my ear
so has your tenderness enfolded me.
No more may I run after the breeze that I most surely
felt
then I may hope to retain the softness of your embrace.
And time looses all seasons as we drift into the
unexplored.
And hopelessly do I cling to the fleeting moments
when our consciousness was but one.

A Summer Evening on Campus

Hands/black hands
Beating against cloth-covered wood
Drumming the sound of urgency
And a kind of complacent happiness
As we sit/sharing the same indignation!
Seeking common entities within ourselves
Gulping to discover those things which are ours —
Our heritage/our black heritage.
Lost in a civilization which our fathers fathered
Yet we remain outcasts.

Blue Because of You

All I know to say I've said.
There remains nothing of doings to do . . . but wait
wait upon time
which in time reveals all things which are.
And should we not be
I will gather all our solemn moments
and tuck them deep into the back of my mind
where time will slowly erase them
until nothing remains but what is
and live forever in a state of oblivion
remembering nothing
while nature nourishes my soul
keeping it as souls are
free from the mask of disguise
that beset the mind of man until it perishes
into a state of uselessness because it clings to
and make idols of those things
that exist not but in the falseness which he contrives.
Today I shall discard forever any future desires I hold
for us
for what will be is already.
Yet vain will I return, as mortals do,
to past events which seemed to hold within the moment
eternity
until time diminishes every fragmentary thought.
Hopelessly, I shall court the memory of you—
Blessing nature that she allowed a mortal like me
to rise above the consciousness of time
to share with you those, now, eternal moments
and until the last ray of light
which shines upon those days and nights

to make them visible in my fading memory.
I shall cherish them and then retire, as seasons do,
to ripen into a fuller and more glorious state
and be all of that which truly is.

Tomorrow

Another week, one more and then what?
Will this burning desire in my heart forever remain?
Your first touch was that which I did not resist.
The second, like a veil of velvet
that colored my thoughts in soft warm hues for an
endless week
until again my eyes beheld you.
And there you were, standing, composed, sure
of what I do not know
while my eyes and mind raced frantically
to discover that thing about you that had captured my
thoughts —
amazed that I, after all, still possessed passion
that so often flees in light of knowledge and reason.
But is there no passion to dissolve in love in light of
reason?
I want to touch you and to feel you close.
O come tomorrow quickly
that I may see who has captured my heart!

The Familiar Face

I don't recall the year
or the season when I first gazed upon his starlit face
but the evening was young as we chattered ceaselessly
into the night.
Nearly like clockwork on certain days we met.
I never thought of him prior to or after we parted.
Upon the changing of circumstances
I not once missed seeing his face nor hearing his voice.
Then one evening when the room could no longer
contain my soul
I left in search of it.
Without a preconceived notion we met in a high school
gymnasium.
As I sat in a futile attempt to feel a part of the game
being played
I glanced about the room and detected upon his face a
radiant look as he came forward.
Together we examined the apathetic faces.
What is it do you suppose
that has befallen the habitants of this great nation of
ours? he asked.
I don't know but my guess would be that it is the lack of
particular stimuli
to create within the urge to seek or to release the
creativity within.
I chuckled upon exclaiming that I was not one
but an affected spectator!
Like a bird with newly clipped wings I was not at all
eager to fly.
The wound, however deep, had not yet closed
from the loss of a love my heart had suffered.
Little if at all would I respond to his tenderness.

I would spend hours forgetting
While being with him.
Even I had begun to think that, alas!
I'd conquered that monstrous villain, Defeat.
Never again would I suffer loss
for never again would I possess.
Without dimly suspecting the consequences I touched
his knee
As I started to pass
and found myself in his embrace.
His face was never again merely a youthful familiar one.
Until he knew I would desire none other he stayed close
by
and then one day as clouds disappear from the sky . . .
he left me.
Last night it rained.

A Dream

Dreamed about a man last night I never even met.
It seemed to me he was in some kind of wreck.
And on my way home I took him with me
to find out later he was great company
and look like to me I don't know from where
but all of a sudden all his clothes were there.
And would you believe I didn't have a grind
about his hanging them right next to mine.
Lord, I was so outdone because I was going say
"Shucks, it's raining so hard now you might as well
stay."
Now you may say that this
is some made-up rhyme
but if I ever see that man
I'm going to know he's mine.

My Lisa

A tear sparkled falling down the cheek of my Lisa.
She is lonely.
The hours find her playing alone with make-believe
people.
Her eyes are like the blaze of burning coal that warms in
winter.
Her limbs — like tender branches of a tree
and her voice echoes through the room as a soft summer
breeze.
Her hair like silk and her smile a blossoming rose.
My Lisa.

Void

I dare not feel as this
listless, void of emotions unimportant
unimpressive as a grain of sand upon the ocean shore.
Soon I shall come alive.
As a bird that awakens with the dawn.
As the sand when sunbeams warm its grain.
As the plant that hasten from the earth to kiss the
sunlight.
As a rosebud that opens to yawn and reveal its beautiful
colors.
As a poet who expresses his/her soul for revitalization.

Dreaming Again

I never knew how much I cared
not that I cared at all
until one day from afar
I saw him standing tall.
I stopped to take a second glance
to see, if by chance,
I was dreaming.
It was real.
Yes, I know today I'll feel his warmth.
But like the sun before the rain
I felt my heart grow fierce with pain.
I was dreaming.

A Tribute to Douglas

Act like you're busy on Mr. Charlie's gig
busy doing anything but learning.
That, he forbids.
The man he'll take one black
aside from all the rest
showing others and the government
at his company even a black can be the best.
Then he watches his little token with dual and foursome
eyes
making sure his little token keeps the company's
standards high.
Though every Chuck and Ann has within their reach a
book
it's only his little token who doesn't dare to take a look.
Because he sees all those eyes
and twice he'd been warned before.
And with Mister Charlie's words on paper
once more, then he's have to go.

September

I remember that evening the sun had set
and darkness had begun to surround us.
You sat at the typewriter working on your first
published article —
I still have a copy —
while I strained my mind and senses
to reach the correct keys on the piano
which were unfamiliar
putting my uppermost thought secondary.
So desperate was I to feel your hands and to kiss your lips.
But some force held me to that piano stool.
We'd said our good-bye long since
The day it ended or the day the words were spoken.
It ended before then.
I was conscious of every moment
wanting to seize the opportunity to be alone with you
wanting to restore what we had lost.
But the crowd who'd gathered to see our show made it
impossible.
Near the middle of that dark, unfinished theater
I found the way to you. I still remember the words.
"Well, I guess this is it," I said.
It's funny now.
You thought I meant the play,
remember?
We were to do it somewhere else.
"Yea, I guess we won't do it again," you replied.
My look turned into a gaze
wishing it was only the show that had ended.
We'd acted as strangers the whole day
and something within me was missing.
I'd built my life around you.

At the end of a workday
seeing you was like a breath of fresh air,
air that now has grown stale.
This month marks one year since then.
The first were frantic months.
I searched vainly for that something to replace the
emptiness,
that longing feeling.
I joined the actor's workshop
to escape being me without you.
Each rehearsal was drudgery
I'd rather have been alone
somewhere isolated with only thoughts of you.
I couldn't bear the reality of you loving another
as you had loved me.
Christmas Eve I remember most vividly.
A huge audience waited
while I, with others, sat backstage
missing that part of me that you once fulfilled.
And when the moment came without jittery nerves
I walked onto that stage
completely unmindful of the audience.
I heard my voice ring loud and clear.
I watched myself make every single move
going into and out of the spotlight
and at the end
I made my face affect a happy look
while inside I bled profusely.
Many hands took hold of mine
congratulating and thanking me
for I don't know what.
I felt twice the emptiness as before.

There was no valid reason
within my reasoning for living another day.
It was early the year that followed
that I rediscovered love
my reason for being.
It's September again
and there are no doors through which I can escape.
Each day marks a year, each moment a week.
You see, again I've lost my reason for being.

Expressions

How many diversions until one reaches the last?
How many ripped dreams and drowned hopes can one
withstand
and still hope and dream?
How many romantic ventures can one fancy
and still hold grip to reality?
How long can synthetics suppress pain?
How long till I give way to loving?
To love a vague possibility
and to spend one's days and nights
acknowledging and courting its improbabilities is a
tortuous thing!
You are my heaven here in hell, or can I no longer
distinguish?
To hear your voice and to look into your eyes set my
soul aflame.
The passion you arouse
is that which addicts seek by injecting poison into their
veins.
It is that which derelicts plunge to the depth of misery
to find
but that which only the strong can win.
Is woman complete without her man?
Or is man given to woman or is woman given to him?
It is to each other that they belong and to whom they give.
Is it love this time?
Or am I falsely pregnant again with passion?
Funny, when I'm with you
my strength becomes its greatest
and when I'm away I weaken.
To me, you're like a strong drug which takes days to
wear off

and when it's gone, I crave another dose.
So then, the question is whether to break the habit
or make sure that it lasts.
How torn am I!
I've long been away
and it is the natural feverish feeling a woman gets when
after many years, she first sees a man
 nothing more; it's all quite natural.
There's nothing to fear, nothing to hope for
nothing that should arouse turmoil. It's all quite natural.
Do I love you? I cannot say.
The years have erased all traces of its meaning.
Perhaps the memory will return. Then I shall answer
you honestly.
But now I only feel the ache inside my head.
Of late, you've taken the place of my alarm clock.
The thought of you awakens me and I lie awake
thinking about you until the alarm rings.
This morning, I kissed the letters which you
with your very own hand had written my name.
 Only a name on a long envelope that I keep near.
Poetry gushes only from the hearts of lovers
for when love is lost the heart is dark and gloomy
and no songs of love are utterable.
If you were married and I were your wife
to know that you had looked at someone
the way you've looked at me
would stir a sickening jealousy within me
which only death could erase.
I simply could not bear those passionate glances given
to anyone but me
if I were her.

Mad? Yes, I surely am to think you could care.
Have two weeks been long?
No, only an eternity.
How did I bear it?
Knowing or imagining you were bearing it too.
Why didn't I call?
I didn't want to reveal to you my weakness.
Why didn't I write?
I would have said too much or not enough.
Too, this whole thing could be but one of my fantasies.
In reality, the two weeks which have passed
you've scarcely thought of me at all.
Is the gap between two races as wide as it appears?
Or is the breach only in the mind and soul?
What happens if both transcend?
What difference is there between two men
one black and one white?
What's the difference if both are scoundrels or wise
men?
Is an honest man none the less if he is black or white —
or the dishonest?
But even an imaginary lover is better than none,
wouldn't you think?
Even sleep to shorten the hours when I shall look upon
your face
plays the cunning trick of evasiveness!
It is better, then, to turn backward and hope to trace
the steps to those I've unwittingly passed than to race
ahead, courageously foolish, to catch a dream.
I've not forgotten your goldfish.
And I'm not unmindful of the fact that you requested
that the color be that of the earrings I wore.

Or was it just a coincidence? Such a sentimental fool I am.
Today I shall visit the aquarium and find a star to place
in your fish bowl.
Despite the battle I fought to retain my heart for
keepsake
all of you it has embraced.
Reject or accept me. The choice is yours.
Tomorrow, will you be wearing that look of confidence
that captured my heart?
At once my heart made a thunderous beat—knowing
that tonight I shall see you.
It is as though someone for whom I've long cared for
has asked me on a date.
More and more I find myself wondering and imagining
what it would be like to make love to you when we
haven't even touched.
Every day I find myself wanting to see you more and
more.
Growing anxiety, isn't that what it is, and not love?
If for once I had time to spare, I would spend it learning
to love you
and discovering all the things that make you happy.
But I keep forgetting. I must remember not to think of
you and not to want you as I do.
I would only be crushed in the end.
Did those words come from you? I do forget.
At the time I must have been in fever, wanting you.
To have gained an inkling of light into the nature of
one's soul and character,
then to take a step backward is to commit moral suicide.
It is human nature to desire the company of others; but
only at times.

In too much company a person is apt to lose sight of himself.

The gap is wider than I thought. To think, we needed an interpreter!

Two people in love who need an interpreter?

Perhaps only one is in love. That must be the case.

I've given to trusting my feelings which is dangerous.
Feelings are misleading. I've often been misled before.

Sometimes I get the feeling that you don't care at all.
Yet, I well know that I cannot wait until Wednesday when we shall meet.

Last night, when I saw you, I was jealous of that someone behind the closed door.

Whenever I see you in that suit, the dark one, you look married. I wonder why?

See how well I'm doing? A whole week, except two days, has passed and I haven't called you once.
See how well I'm doing?

If I call, for sure you'll know how desperate I am to see you

and to see you only prolongs my agony.

But at this moment I would choose dying to not seeing you at all.

I need you to talk to. But more than anything, I need you to love.

I am nervously weak.

It might soon happen that I shall have to stop seeing you abruptly.

This day seems endless.

Tonight I will see you and more than likely leave more assured that this feeling I have for you is the product of my imagination

though it all seems so real.
The other night I did get closer to you, even though it was just a dream.
You lay beside me while neither of us touched. We played the game of love with someone else.
But we both knew it was only a game.
My true love I had given to you.
Could it be that I am a fanatic lover?
If there was not man with his splendor, I would embrace the trees.
Do people in love, in time, grow tired of each other?
I would like to grow tired and old with you.
I am now dreaming of the day when we'll help each other to climb the stairs to our bedroom. And when we reach it, we'll both be out of breath.
We'll smile—remembering the days when we had raced up the stairs.
We'll both be glad that those times are behind us.
Yesterday I began learning to forget you.
It is true. I have come to love you because you are a symbol
holding a light to lead to understanding my past.
Without a dream of the future I would be lost!
I haven't thought about you much. Neither have you occupied a place in my dreams.
At this moment I'm feeling better; almost as though I could live without your love.
Love must be seasonal and this is its time.
Learning that you don't love me has enhanced my feelings for you. Now thrice the distance is between us.
To lose strength and courage now would be as saying it all rested with you

when not long ago we met. If it is so, then before, I was without courage and strength
and that is not entirely true.
I do wish you loved me. It's wonderful to love
but I think to be loved, too, is a marvelous thing.
To escape reality is to think you do love me.
But it is only with what is real, concrete, that I will build my future.
You say you don't love me and that I must accept it.
Tonight I shall see you, knowing well that you don't love me. It won't be hard at all.
I've loved you since the first time I perceived that you could care for me.
Maybe one day you might call.
Is it better to have loved and lost than never to have loved at all?
Time has a way of making all big things look small, and maybe vice versa.
When I first saw you I thought with assurance, "I won't fall in love."
This morning it appears that this torch I've been carrying in my heart for you is cooling.
These days the thought of death is pleasant because to love is painful.
To escape to find a moment of bliss is worth all the hours in a day.
My heart is buried in apathy.
To live without love is to live without food and drink.
I'm dying of starvation and thirst!
To crave for the ideal is a yoke upon those who hunger after it.
They move forward in pain and in agony.

My feelings are numb. I neither desire nor repel you.
Yesterday, I loved you more than ever.
Once you said that this love I feel could not be for you at
all.
If that is true, the remainder of my life I shall spend
looking for the person for whom it is meant. I will go
out of my way to find him as I did last week when
someone from my past came to mind.
I rushed to him, wondering if he were the one. He was
not.
I must continue to search my memory or that part which
still remains.
What will happen if I never find him?
It is early afternoon now and tonight I will see you.
If I believed in gods, I would ask them to help me to
forget about you
 if no more than to deceive them all.
I love you and haven't the slightest desire to forget you.
I know you don't love me, and probably never could.
Am I boisterous and bold? If so, do you like these
qualities in a woman?
Too bad I cannot change to suit you. But I'm glad
for that person to whom this love is meant will love me
not just for what I am, but for what I could and someday
will be:
 a virtuous woman, loyal to her own convictions and to
her man.
For the time I'll have to give up the thought of forgetting
you
because today I've hardly thought of anybody else.
Last night I watched your face go flush when I said that
another man had kissed me

and I saw the excitement which stirred in you at the
realization that someone else had loved me.
I've grown to expect seeing you with vigor, even
knowing that
to you, it's not at all so personal.
I wonder, too, if you've thought about me since last
Wednesday.
Today I'm certain that you think of me too. I think you
could care deeply.
Perhaps my fantasies are growing again.
It could be true that I don't love you.
But that truth, if it is so, is now to my thinking a
falsehood.
I care more than perhaps I ought.
Today I pick up my pen with disgust for this apathy
within me
like wanting to sleep my life away
like nothing is worth wishing and fighting for
like life for me is doomed to shallow misery
like life is useless and happiness impossible!
I consider myself lucky today to have an idea to love
even though it may be false. But I cannot live without
love!
I'm going to leave you because I must — and because I
love you.
I will die of this wound rather than continue to bleed.
Yet, I well know I'll die a thousand deaths when I leave
and still continue to live.
It's all happening as I thought.
Oh, how lonely I will be.
I love you so indiscriminately.
How do I begin to free my mind of thoughts of you?

I've been afflicted by a plague which is instilled into the
very air I breathe.
I'm sick with love for you.
Still I go around pretending that I'm well and healthy
while inside I'm dying that I may live again
to receive a love that may be shared by both.
Each time I visit you and the door at the end of the
corridor is opened
I somehow identify with that dreadfully empty room.
But then, the thought that I'm just a few feet away from
you
fills me with a kind of gladness that I've escaped that
room.
While looking at the room, I think of loving you.
You remind me of no one else I know.
Last night I dreamed about you
dreamed I loved you as much as I do when I'm awake.
I cannot tear away from you, not just yet.
It is my own weakness and fear
fear that this fantasy might drown. And shouldn't it?
Since it is what it is. Even my answer is yes.
But just a little longer I want to fancy that it is possible
For me to share a larger portion of your life and you
mine.
You couldn't have meant what you said about seeing
me personally.
Surely it was a slip of the tongue. You meant privately,
didn't you?
There's a vast difference. You meant privately, I'm sure.
How is one to describe numbness?
No sorrow, no hope, no wishing you wouldn't go
no hoping you'll stay.

I'll miss you, I'm sure, when my feelings return.
You were my hope for light in absolute darkness.
Don't leave me now!
When I see you soon for the last time
I'll act a heroic role as though I'll be happy —
 No, not happy but pleased that you're leaving.
What month is it now?
June — it's the middle of it.
I will tear myself free of all thought of you
except that you are warm and most kind.
I will fill the emptiness of the days we used to meet.
Today, it's more like an unclear dream that you're going away.
It is this need I have for you now of which I spoke in answer to your statement
"He must have loved you very much."
No, my love, he didn't love me. But he needed me, just as I need you.
You will leave soon, and I must manage my life without you.
I cannot think of you for long
else I sink into a well of pity and make a spectacle of my tears.
You are going away. Will you write once, then never again?
Tomorrow I will see you for the last time.
I wonder if you wanted to say yes to the dinner invitation.
And if so, what prevented you?
Could you be leaving because of me?
Was that a look of love you gave me last evening?
This emptiness is unbearable!

Another Dream

Last night I dreamed I loved you. It was strange.
Just when I was thinking deeply of you, you appeared.
I apologized to you for something I felt guilty of.
You assured me of your love. There was music, song,
laughter, and there were tears.
I held your head close to my breast.
There was great warmth in my heart for you.
Then you said you didn't care.
We sought different partners until once again we could
both feel the warmth.

Blowing the Top Off the World

I'm gonna blow the top right off this world.
Blowing the top off the world so I can see what's
beneath.
Then I'll know whether it should've stayed on after all.

Don't Look at Me That Way

Don't look at me that way
I remember, he used to look at me that way.
I would feel exposed and, at the same time, afraid.
Afraid that others would notice and for some reason
I didn't want others to know how he felt about me.
He looked at me that way until I could not resist,
resist succumbing to the desire I felt to be closer,
closer to him to talk with him.
And when I could not conceal my feelings for him
he withdrew himself away from me.
Don't look at me that way because,
because this time, I'll not give away to the emotion.
Then you will not withdraw away from me because,
because you will never know that I read in your eyes
that you could care.

On Man and Woman

Everything has already been said and written about
man and woman and their attraction for one another.
What then is left to say about you and me?
The bond between us is fragile.
 As though a single thought could fragment and disrupt
it all.
I think of you and then I see you
and wonder how I ever developed the courage to
approach you.
Fear of rejection was and continues to be strong.
But you respond warmly to my awkward gestures.
You keep me waiting until my patience grows thin
but for now there's no other thing to do but to wait.
What is this bond and of what does it consist?
For me it is a passion I feel for life
which you have restored
An excitement that stirs my heart and surrounds it with
warmth
and a longing to be near.

Elegy for John

John, our friend, today, we're missing you. Our hearts
are filled with grief.
Never again will we laugh and talk and play the way
we used to.
John, our friend, the embodiment of the struggling
musician-artist
whose heart was big and warm.
The struggling musician-artist who had little
save himself, but that he had completely.
A self no one of us could conquer or possess completely.
John, our friend, you hid your pain and sorrow behind a
smile so endearing
and a touch so warm.
No one knew of your inner suffering and pain.
You were careful not to share with us your grief.
But we knew, John, although you never told us.
We knew because we felt your soul, your spirit.

About Miles

Miles flying high in the sky
riding the souls of thousands of others
making us feel good, good, good.
Blow your horn, Miles.
Blow till I forget my troubles.
Blow 'till my soul soars with yours.
Yeah, like that.
Now ease me down just so.
Yes, like that.
Okay, baby, you're on your own now solo.
Ummm, so mellow, impetuous, outrageous.
Frantic! Now softly, gently gentle, suave.

To Miles

I wanna shout to the world
but they won't stop to hear.
Wanna tell 'em how you move my soul
beyond any planet near.
Gotta tell 'em with words
how your music makes me feel.
Yet every attempt
makes it all seem unreal.
Because there are no phrases to confirm what I know is
true
I'll just have to spend my life loving you
Silently, passionately.

For Miles

Through the years I've grown nearly as quiet as you
and my habit of brooding has become as persistent as
yours.
There were times when I forgot the feel of a smile upon
my face.
Blocks of uncertainties clouded the light
making it difficult to see the way.
Today I'm as blue as your title tune, "All Blues"
when only yesterday I was so happy.
My heart and soul sang the song of love and life.
As evening slowly disappears
I'm wondering in what mood I'll spend the oncoming
night.
I detest these moments
when my very soul seems to drag the bottomless
pyramid.
Is it this low ebb
that causes our hearts to rejoice so clingingly when it
reaches the top?
Is it our destiny to inevitably witness in moments of
silence
the bewitching secrets of loneliness?
Or shall we ever know of our oneness with each other
 realizing only our consciousness of time and space
separate us?
It's blissful to have known you
when time was of no essence and space could not
occupy our thoughts.
You and I alone in silence; there were no need for words
we both knew.

A Tribute to Those with Nowhere to Go and No Time to Be There

Nowhere to go and no time to be there.
What then is left to do but heckle me to make their presence felt
the way I do with my writing?
I wonder if my presence felt is of delight, fright,
annoyance, or grace.
Do I prey upon others the way those with nowhere to
go and no time to be there prey upon me?
All I want is never to have to deal with
to be aware of or to be near, in any way,
those with nowhere to go and no time to be there.
They can be heard coming and going for blocks away.
Their sensitivity has been destroyed. They act without
feeling.
People who have nowhere to go and no time to be there,
this is my tribute to you.
This is to let you know as you have made sure
I hear you.
You have gotten through to me.
You have made your presence felt.
I am tired of your world.
I do not wish to share my world with you any longer.
Let me assure you,
people with nowhere to go and no time to be there,
I will make my escape.
Somehow, I will escape from the torture you have
inflicted upon me.
Somehow, I will get from under your spell.
One day I will not be the subject of your violent cut-off
selves.
You people with nowhere to go and no time to be there,
your actions have been instruments of torment

because you have been cut off from yourselves and your
sensitivity has been destroyed.
One day,
mark my word,
I will escape from this den into which I've been held
captive.
One day you will pay for your crimes of torture,
and the price will be mine to ask!

A Poem

A Poem. What is it?
Must a poem be universal in nature to be a poem?
Should most people have experienced the experience
written about?
The years have erased one kind of misery and replaced
it with another.
It used to be that I would think myself complete
if only there was someone who could care and share a
portion of my life.
Now, it doesn't matter much whether anyone cares.
All that is important now
is that the hours in the day be filled with activity.
I'm not even particular about the kind of activity so long
as it is not destructive in nature.
Though I would prefer activity which is engaging and
interesting
I'd settle, for a while, with anything—
filing, posting, cleaning drawers, or just anything.
A Poem. What is it?
Is it a bundle of disillusions or contradictions
or carefully worded phrases that express these feelings?
And what is there to be said of disillusion and how have
I become so?
At first I thought that if one applied oneself
to the process of self-improvement
things would begin to happen that would lend support
to the idea.
That one's position in the world would move up, as an
example.
Or that success or reward cannot come to those who do
not seek or endeavor to make success a realization.
That, neither, is true.

For symbolism's reward or success is given to one by his/her benefactor
whose criterion for selection is determined by those who support his/her (benefactor's) own sense of life and values
which can be and often is a separate reality than what exists.
The benefactor selects those who help him/her to reaffirm his/her own identity and sense of life. Success and reward is separate, and apart from performance or one's ability to perform,
the contradictions are there undeniably. Not a contradiction in itself but a contradiction in what I had perceived to be a reality.

On the Job

I wonder what sitting idle does for a person.
You can't read or write because it's on company time.
I think it must make one dumb.
And even dumber is the person(s) who makes such
rules.
It suits them fine to see a worker idle and afraid to do
anything
other than company business, even though there's no
company business to do.
I have now a magazine that I wouldn't mind browsing
through . . .
but it's company time
and ever so often
the "top dog" comes out of his house to see to it that
if there's nothing to do nothing is being done.
It suits him fine that way.
Do nothing. Say nothing. Be nothing unless you want
trouble.
Unless you want trouble
you'd better not look like you're doing something
if there's nothing to do.

Waiting

Foolish or wise am I to wait for a call which may not
come . . .
To wait for someone who may not be there or here.
And if I decide not to wait
would my actions/thoughts be different than what they
are?
The magic is waning . . .
Those moments we spent together are becoming the
moments of two mere mortals.
And what of those moments?
They were as though you and I were the only persons
upon the earth.
No, they were as though the inevitable had happened.
The strain of waiting and all the uncertainties laid to
rest.
But just for those few moments because soon after the
parting
doubt and fear are reborn anew.
If I were not waiting for you
my time would be spent as usual in isolation
without the luring hope that love brings
and without future dreams of happiness.
 Without the ecstasy of the thought of you
I would not fear the thought of falling into despair
because in despair I would live.
The idea that you may call or may be there
postpones for a while the inevitable visit of my desolate
companion:
loneliness.

For Steve

When I was fulfilled and complete within myself and
had no want of anyone
you appeared, as though from a mist
and awakened in me desire which I feel for you.
Now, when you're gone and I must become as I was—
fulfilled and complete within myself—
I become anxious about whether you'll be there.
Then you appeared, as though from a mist.
Though you cannot trust me with your intimate self
and keep me at a distance safe it's okay.
Perhaps I've been there too.
And when you're near
I'm overwhelmed with passion and I experience you as
love.
Love that comes and possesses me for a while.
Now I need to do what, alone, I cannot.
Stir my emotions until they burst inside
and spread throughout the universe like a panacea
for all to experience to feel the warmth, the beauty that
loving creates.
You found and reawakened a part of me that was in
darkness
until you appeared out of the mist.
If the future will put us together or take us apart I
cannot know.
But now you are there and I am here
until need and desire bridge the chasm
and again I experience you next to me as love.

A Summer Dream

This morning when I awoke I heard the soft singing of
birds outside my window
 before the break of dawn.
The streets were quiet of rushing cars
the sidewalk empty of moving feet.
No sound of children playing
no running water from faucets next door.
Softly and quietly was the beginning of a dream
which will not live through winter.
It will fade like flowers at the end of season.
 Like trees, that shed their leaves in autumn for the new.
Like hearts that break to be mended.
Like rainbows that vanish with clearing skies.
It was the beginning of spring.

About Us

If I could write a poem today it would be about us
and how we once were, you and I.
It shines deep in my memory
like the morning sun.
I see us together, you and I
as though the years that separate us never really were.
The only bind between us is our thought about each
other
you and I. Without it there is nothing.
Then there was our togetherness.
Now we both have the thought of that.
There is no desire by either of us to make it more than
what it is
a light which will not fade or diminish; it is just there
like the morning sun.
If I could write a poem today it would be about us
about how you made me feel when we were *together*.
It has never left me
through all the years gone by.
You were everything to me for just a little while.
For the first time I felt whole
as though you were the part of me that was missing.
Hard as I try
I cannot remain neutral whenever you are near.
Either I'm sad, glad, hurt, or mad.
You stir emotions I cannot suppress.
If I could write a poem today
it would be about us
about how the thought of you moves me to laughter, to
tears.
It would be about the morning sun.

Impossible

I wish I'd not seen you.
I wouldn't now be disappointed at not seeing you.
It is true you are but an image of my idea of man.
You won't come today, I know you won't but still I wish
wish to hear your voice
to see your body's shape
your unseen feet that form the shape of your shoes.
Now I have seen your face and heard your voice
and that, alone, does not satisfy
but leaves me with even a stronger longing
to speak to you of your personal convictions
which you must surely possess
else you could not walk as you walk
or speak the tone of voice in which you speak.
Quickly, I must learn not to think of you
for then I am reminded of the impossibility of our
getting together.
Two unapproachable worlds separate us.
A wall stands too high to climb
or we lick the ground with our bellies to cross beneath
and having crossed which of us will take sides?
The thought of you leaves me weak.
I must pretend as I pass you
that you're an unimportant representation
of what man should be and struggle to keep composed.
How I *wish* just to see you!
If it is possible to love someone then I love you . . .
Yes, I do love all that I see of you
and despise my weakness for having loved you
hopelessly.
Despise my longing to be near you
just to see you!

At evening time I will think of you and the impossibility
of our getting together.
Maybe tomorrow I'll be stronger realizing and accepting
that having you is impossible.
If just knowing that you're near
within these same walls
breathing the same air is as near as I'll ever be to you
then I should begin to be content.
But still I wish
wish by chance we could chance to be close
closer than just sharing the same hours in the same
building
seeing the same faces and during this time
which I hope to be short
that this building should contain the two of us at once.
I wish the chance to glance upon you in passing.
I've given up the idea of speaking
for our eyes cannot meet for long else we both pretend
not to see.
As a secret promise
Each day I will think of as many ways as possible
for my mind to dream up to get nearer you
and wish often to see you passing, pretending you don't
see.
You've made your choice. You are the wise one.
You will not jeopardize your status in your world to
enter mine.
In your world your chances for "success" are excellent
whereas in mine it would be impossible
except measured by my own standards.
You don't pass my way now.
You don't have to pretend

making it easier in the end for me.
Impossible!
You cannot make it easy for me
until I know that you are not as I think you are
and to know that
I must first know you and I shall never know you.
I would leave my fate to chance just to know you.
But I cannot expect so much from you.
You have found no excuse to pass my way today
and maybe the other days you passed were not as an
excuse.
And maybe you've not seen me after all.

A Black Soul Cries

Feel my soul, my sensitivity, my heart crying for
tenderness.
You hurt me deeper than anyone else ever could.
No load is too heavy.
If I show weakness you beat me unsympathetically.
Yet a moment of your kindness is worth all of the
goodness of a lifetime.
You cause me to live in constant fear.
Fear of breaking
and fear of the bigness and the strength of your hands,
your fist . . .
Fear that only another will know your tenderness
and the extent of your kindness.
You don't know the softness beneath my rough-looking
complexion.
I feel all things.
 When you touch me I may not feel as soft cotton or
velvet
but I feel you.

You slap my face
close your fingers tight, hit me anywhere.
I feel that too
long after the pain is gone.
Yet within your arms for a single moment
is worth a lifetime of someone else's giving.

Black and Poor

To be born black and poor
is to know the rawness of being hated,
treated with contempt and scorn.
It is to know with ease the feeling of being cramped in
too small a place.
Knowing the stink of rancid grease,
thinking that a roach rightly belongs in kitchens or
anywhere else it decides to crawl.
Being black and poor is to know too well the sound of
tiny feet of mice
scurrying their way about.
To be born black and poor
is to know how it feels to have a bill collector attach
your not-enough-money anyway
or to wear a pair of shoes until the soles flap.
The times I've worn cardboard!
Early in life, if you're smart,
you learn to be good
and being good means
to accept without question what they tell you
about how Lincoln and all the rest of the slave owners
did so much for you
and when you learn it was all lies you've been told and
develop a yearning
unabated desire to find out the truth, you become a
"troublemaker,"
or a "Black Militant," or even a "Panther,"
just because, in your search for truth
you discover there's something as good in you as there
is in anyone.
When you go to find a job
somehow you already know before you get there

that the opening was "just filled."
So you try real hard to find a positive approach to life
to ward off the sickening glances you get
when you go to the beach to feel the fresh air just off the
ocean
and to enjoy that life-giving substance, the sun.
You lie there in the sand
and for just a short moment you forget the burdens you
carry for being born black
until you hear someone passing by mumbling, "She's
dark enough already."
God, they think even the sun is all theirs!
If you're black you have no right to take off your shoes
(if you have any)
to feel the sand beneath your feet.
If you're black you have no right to be a human being.
You live to have a family
and if you're lucky, as I am,
you learn to love,
and being the victim of hate,
gradually, you develop a compassion for the opposite.

Love Lost

Living in this society
that has forsaken and bypassed
the source from which flows the strength and vitality of
life
today's actions manifest a time when the soul of man is
so tortured
that only insaneness soothes.
And I see the loneness of a single being
reaching out—stopping anyone who will
clinging to strangers crying
pleading for a moment of that something
that will lend the soul nourishment—Truth
and only the very young at heart can respond.

Youth and Old Age

While the envy of youth feast upon my soul
I'm suspended between heaven and hell.
Heaven — loving that which has quelled the madness of
my youth.
Hell — age that has stamped out that fervent desire to
roam.
Detesting the obedience of the heart that tolerates
what time has forced upon it.
And there's naught to comfort but memories
of stolen loves and captured ones.
Now there's no heaven or hell
but a void which makes me unfamiliar
with those most common things I fancied knowing at
other times.
Now I'm without love, hate, hope, or despair
like a particle of dust seen only through a ray of
sunlight.

I Like Jazz

I like jazz music because it says in rhythm what I feel: struggle, triumph, defeat, joy, sorrow . . . serenity. Jazz music and I are one.

To Emery

Funny with all the talk today about people loving
people, black power, and people joining together
when mothers and daughters and lovers
still find no grounds upon which they can lay down
their pretensions
to be only themselves.
And time is not still long enough for lovers to convey
love
because in another moment it is foreign.
So it is through a power within that we relate
and through that power (emotions) mothers relate,
daughters relate, and lovers relate.
Too often are words misinterpreted and actions
misleading.

My Beginning

When first my childhood cares were few
I played among animals and listened, enchantingly, to
singing birds.
And when the season was right
found nuts under the leaves of old hickory trees and ate
until filled.
From among the sharpest thorn were found the sweetest
berries.
At nightfall, when the moon was high and stars were
bright
I lay close to the open window and of some distant
future I would dream.
Then I was nearest to heaven.
I could see plainly the moonlight shining down between
the tall pines
which at night stood high
and I was drawn by my childhood fantasies
to become absorbed into that existence
and in the darkness silently I cried out.
At the break of dawn
when roosters crowed through my windowpane
the early morning sun would beckon me
and with great haste I rushed to it.
And now I'm consumed by madness.

We'll Be Together Again

O stars above, please let me know
am I insane to want him so?
From the time we first did meet
I knew my heart was his to keep.
In all the years he was away
my heart so little did go astray.
And when he's near I still do hear
my heart beat strongly—my love, my dear!
And when time itself will for us cease to be
somewhere together we'll be—I and thee.
O stars above, only you can know
when this want within will be no more.

Being Black

Being black is always being suspicious if someone's out to hurt you
both from within and from without.
It's feeling the peculiar pain of being the object of hatred — often impersonal.
Being black is feeling ashamed of yourself
for what you've not been able to accomplish — the American dream.
Being black is praying forgiveness for imperfections
made to feel small and insignificant as a person.
(God, I'm so imperfect!)
My name has changed so often
I hope I don't forget who I am.
But then I think, "I don't care what you call me, just 'long as you call me."
Being black is like living in a constant state of emergency
always being aggravated by something or the other
always something needs fixing
something that must be taken care of right away — like survival.
Being black means living in seclusion
and learning to accept what was so painful to discover.
It's learning to create from nothing.
Being black is challenging!

Computerization

Jammed up
compartmentalized and unable to function outside
myself.
Choked, strangled
cut off from all things bad, small, and large.
Existing in a vacuum unable to breathe air from
without.
Am I suffocating?
Looks like it, feels like it.
I'm dead but yet unburied.
No hope
tired of trying
giving in to nonfeeling
nonloving, noncaring.
Entering the noncompassionate side of life
where nothing hurts and nothing feels good.
Just being.

The World Gets Along Without Me Very Well

Productivity is up, unemployment is down
but I'm still around seeking ways to expand on nothing.
Art is flourishing, creativity abounds
among artists, scientists.
Politicians are parading their potentials
but they all get along without me.
I watch the world go by, go-round
 and when I try to jump on . . .
I realize I'm out of step and miss each time.
Friends go on being friendly
lovers, loving players, playing
no one notices I've dropped out.
News goes on being told.
Any young people growing old?
It all goes on without mine being told.
Cars and people go by
airplanes and helicopters fly
actors are acting, the famous are dying, and human
feelings abound.
No one notices I'm not around.
Yes, the world gets along without me very well.

The End

CPSIA information can be obtained at www.ICGtesting.com
Printed in the USA
BVOW041734151111

276150BV00001B/105/P